The Triangle Shirtwaist
Factory Fire

Adam R. Schaefer

WORLD ALMANAC® LIBRARY

Please visit our web site at: www.worldalmanaclibrary.com
For a free color catalog describing World Almanac® Library's list of high-quality
books and multimedia programs, call 1-800-848-2928 (USA) or 1-800-387-3178
(Canada). World Almanac® Library's fax: (414) 332-3567.

Library of Congress Cataloging-in-Publication Data

Schaefer, Adam R., 1976-
  The Triangle Shirtwaist Factory fire / by Adam R. Schaefer.
    p. cm. — (Landmark events in American history)
  Summary: Explains the circumstances that led to the tragic 1911 garment factory
fire that killed 146 people, examines the role of unions and reformers, and details how
public opinion eventually forced state governments to legislate for safe working conditions.
  Includes bibliographical references and index.
  ISBN 0-8368-5383-0 (lib. bdg.)
  ISBN 0-8368-5411-X (softcover)
  1. Triangle Shirtwaist Company—Fire, 1911—Juvenile literature. 2. New York (N.Y.)—
History—1898-1951—Juvenile literature. 3. Clothing factories—New York (State)—New
York—Safety measures—History—20th century—Juvenile literature. 4. Labor laws and
legislation—New York (State)—New York—History—20th century—Juvenile literature.
[1. Triangle Shirtwaist Company—Fire, 1911. 2. Industrial safety—History.] I. Title.
II. Series.
F128.5.S34   2003
974.7'1041—dc21   2003047946

First published in 2004 by
World Almanac® Library
330 West Olive Street, Suite 100
Milwaukee, WI 53212 USA

Produced by Discovery Books
Editor: Sabrina Crewe
Designer and page production: Sabine Beaupré
Photo researcher: Sabrina Crewe
Maps and diagrams: Stefan Chabluk
World Almanac® Library editorial direction: Mark J. Sachner
World Almanac® Library art direction: Tammy Gruenewald
World Almanac® Library production: Beth Meinholz and Jessica Yanke

Photo credits: Corbis: pp. 4, 9, 13, 18, 21, 27; The Granger Collection: pp. 11,
12, 40, 41; Kheel Center, Cornell University: pp. 17, 19, 20, 22, 24, 25, 26, 29, 30,
31, 32, 33, 34, 35, 36, 37, 39; Library of Congress: p. 7; NYU/Ken Levinson: cover,
p. 42; North Wind Picture Archives: pp. 5, 6, 8, 10, 14, 15, 16, 28, 38; UNITE: p.43.

Printed in the United States of America

1 2 3 4 5 6 7 8 9 07 06 05 04 03

Contents

Introduction

This advertisement for dressmaking patterns from around 1900 shows (far right) a lady's shirtwaist of the period. A shirtwaist tucked into a long skirt was a very popular style of dress.

The End of the Working Day

March 25, 1911, was a typical Saturday afternoon at the Triangle factory. The factory was housed on the top three floors of the Asch building in New York City. It was a clothing factory that made shirtwaists, a popular style of everyday blouse for women in the early twentieth century.

Inside the building, workers were preparing to go home at the end of a long day. Most of them were young women and girls, recent **immigrants** from Europe, between the ages of thirteen and twenty-three years old.

Trapped by Fire

Before the workers could leave, a fire broke out on the eighth floor of the building and spread to the floors above. Firefighters got to the building as quickly as they could, but they could do little to help the people inside. The fire pressed relentlessly against the trapped workers, who began to jump from windows to the sidewalk below. They were watched by a horrified crowd on the street.

This was not the worst fire the people of New York City had ever seen, but the loss of human life was devastating. Nearly 150 men and women, employees of the Triangle Shirtwaist Factory, died as a result of the fire that day.

A view of New York City in about 1900 shows the towering skyscrapers in which many people worked. Most of these buildings would have been death traps if a fire broke out.

No Regulation

The public was outraged that the factory owners had done nothing to protect the workers. At the time, safety measures in factories were almost nonexistent. The government did not **regulate** business, believing it did not have the power to interfere. The situation had been going on for some time, and people known as **reformers** had already spoken out about the problems and dangers.

After the Triangle fire, state governments could no longer ignore the need to involve themselves in the regulation of factories. The fire had made it clear that safety and health at work were being denied to millions of hardworking people in factories. Dozens of new laws were soon passed, requiring businesses to maintain safer working conditions or face being shut down.

Chapter 1

The Move to the Cities

Farm Country

The United States started as a nation of farmers. There were some cities, but they were not the large business centers they are today, and there were no factories. People worked with their families on farms, and they did not need other jobs to make money. In the early 1800s, most families could not afford to send children to school, but school was not considered essential because people did not need an education to get a job in an agricultural society.

Rapid Change and Growth

Before the mid-1800s, there was little manufacturing industry, other than **textile** factories, because most items people needed were still made at home or on a small, local scale. After the Civil War, things began to change. The war ended in 1865, and the United States entered a period of rapid **industrialization**. The

The steel industry became the backbone of the Industrial Revolution. Huge steelworks sprang up around U.S. cities, transforming farmland into a landscape of large, smoky factories.

Industrial Revolution took hold as one development fueled another. New technology brought new products, which needed to be manufactured for mass consumption. Iron and steel were produced in huge quantities to build railroads across the nation. The railroads opened up new opportunities to move people and goods around the country. This, in turn, created new or increased demands: for building materials, for fuel such as coal and oil, for new machines, and for packaged and processed foods.

The Demand for Workers

Factories and businesses sprang up, rushing to fulfill the growing demands. This led to yet another need, one for a huge workforce to labor in the factories. Factory owners sent agents to Europe to convince poor Europeans that new and better jobs were waiting for them in the United States. Between 1865 and 1873, about 3 million immigrants came to the United States, lured by the offer of jobs and the opportunity to escape from overcrowded European cities. As

Rapid Changes
"There is nothing in all the past to compare with the rapid changes now going on in the civilized world. . . . The snail's pace . . . has suddenly become the headlong rush of the locomotive, speeding faster and faster."

Henry George, Social Problems, *1883*

immigrants filled the cities and factories, industrial workers began to outnumber agricultural workers for the first time.

Workers Flood to the Cities

In the late 1800s, millions of immigrants continued to arrive in the United States, expecting a better life than the one they had left behind. Most of these immigrants were uneducated and hoping only to find unskilled manufacturing work. They crowded into the cities where factories were springing up.

At the same time, American inventors were introducing new agricultural machines that could do the work of many farmers. Landowners did not need as many agricultural workers as before,

Helping the Industrial Revolution

Eli Whitney (1765–1825) twice played a vital role in advancing the American Industrial Revolution. In 1793, he built a cotton gin, a machine that could clean cotton fifty times faster than a person could by hand. By 1840, as a result, the United States was producing 60 percent of the world's processed cotton.

In 1800, Eli Whitney started making interchangeable parts—he built guns made of replaceable pieces instead of hand-crafting each gun individually. Soon, many factories started using interchangeable parts for their machines and their products. The age of mass production had begun.

Eli Whitney's cotton gin, an early development of the Industrial Revolution.

and so unemployed farm laborers moved to the cities to work in factories. The cities quickly swelled with the arrival of so many new residents from abroad and from rural areas.

Another addition to the workforce was women. In the past, most women had worked at home, but now they began working in factories and shops. Women were paid less than male employees even though they worked as many hours and just as hard as men.

Crowded Conditions

The majority of newcomers to the city lived in high-story **tenement** houses, built rapidly—and badly—in response to the demand for additional housing. These buildings were extremely overcrowded, sometimes with ten or fifteen people living and sleeping in one small room. The rooms were dark, and some did not even have windows. Rats and insects crawled on the floors where people slept.

This busy intersection in Chicago in 1909 shows that there were traffic jams even before there were cars. New forms of transportation, such as cable cars and trains, created new industries and helped workers get to their jobs.

Tenement Life

Immigrants were desperately poor and could not afford to eat healthy food. As a result, many people became **malnourished**. Sickness and disease raged through the tenements, causing thousands of people to die. Doctors had not yet discovered cures or vaccinations for the many illnesses killing the tenement dwellers. Most immigrant workers could not afford to pay for doctors or medical treatment anyway.

Pollution became a problem in American cities for the first time. The best tenement houses had two toilets on each floor, while some had just one in a courtyard at the bottom of the building. The landlords did not properly dispose of waste—a fact that helped many diseases spread easily.

The working poor of the late 1800s and early 1900s lived in desperate conditions in city tenements. Crime and disease flourished, and there was no way out of the misery for most people.

Utter Wretchedness and Misery

". . . half a million men, women and children are living in the tenement houses of New York. . . . No brush could paint or pencil describe . . . the utter wretchedness and misery, the vice and crime, that may be found within a stone's throw of City Hall, even within an arm's length of many churches. . . . From the nearly 200,000 tenement houses come 93 percent of the deaths and 90 percent of the crimes of our population."

Harper's Weekly *magazine, 1876*

The Factories

Living in the city in the late 1800s was very unpleasant, but working in a factory was even more so. When factories first appeared in the United States, they were often safer and cleaner than the ones in Europe. Soon, however, factory owners had many potential employees to choose from, more than they could ever possibly use. They realized they did not need safe factories to entice new employees. As a result, working conditions became much worse, and it did not take long before the American factories were just as dangerous and unhealthy as the ones in Europe.

Factories generally had bad **ventilation** and no heating. They were overcrowded with people, equipment, and materials, which made them vulnerable to fire and accidents. People had to operate dangerous machinery with no safety devices, and they were frequently injured and even killed. There were not many toilets in the factories, and employees were rarely allowed to use them during working hours. **Unsanitary** conditions caused workers to get sick, but they could not afford to stay home, and so illness spread throughout the factory.

The Rules of Work

In these horrible conditions, people were required to work as many hours and days as their employers demanded, or they would lose

Processed food was an innovation of the late 1800s, and demand for it grew along with city populations. In this crowded factory, women and children are preparing vegetables for canning.

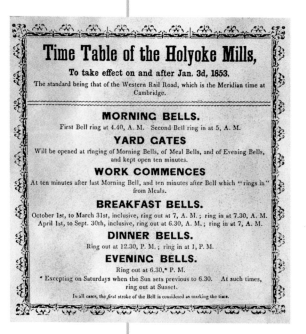

A factory timetable from 1853 shows that people were expected to work from 5:00 A.M. to 6:30 P.M. except on Sundays. They were, however, given two half-hour meal breaks, which became less common as manufacturing industry in the United States progressed and factory conditions got worse.

their jobs. Workers were not paid for overtime because there was no such thing as overtime. They did not receive a break for lunch, but sometimes they were allowed to eat something that they had brought from home. They might be required to work on Sundays even though many of them were strongly religious. Sometimes, workers were fired for being late just one time.

Supervisors watched employees closely to make sure they were working at all times. Workers were followed and rushed when they went to the bathroom to make sure they did not take extra breaks. Supervisors were so concerned about employees stealing

Minimum Wages and Working Hours

Today, there is a minimum wage in the United States. A minimum wage is the least amount of money that workers must be paid, per hour, according to the law. The minimum wage is not the same in every state because it costs more to live in some places than others. Not everyone receives the minimum wage, however, even today. Many people, especially recent immigrants, still work for less than the minimum wage because they need the work so badly. Certain jobs, such as that of a server in a restaurant, do not pay a minimum wage because earnings are supplemented with tips.

In the United States, a standard workweek is forty hours. Employees are paid extra for working more than forty hours in one week, and this is called overtime. Someone who normally makes $10 per hour is usually paid $15 per hour for their overtime hours. But even today, the poorest people in society often work without overtime bonuses.

supplies or products that they often searched the workers when they left at the end of the day.

It was not just adults who had to labor in these awful circumstances. Children also had to work if their families were to scrape by. By the mid-1800s, there were laws in some states that limited the hours worked by small children, but they were often ignored. Children as young as six years old toiled alongside adults in factories and were expected to work just as long and hard.

Scraping By

In the late 1800s, industry boomed, businessmen got rich, and yet living and working conditions for the **urban** poor became worse. The government did not set a minimum wage, and employers could pay workers as little as they wanted. American factory owners quickly discovered they could pay immigrant employees even less than American-born workers. Immigrants were accustomed to working for very little money in their home countries, and they knew if they did not take a low-paying job, someone else would. It was better to have a low-paying job than no job at all.

Children from poor families were cheap labor as far as the factory owners of the late 1800s and early 1900s were concerned. These children are working the spinning machines in a textile factory.

13

The Struggle for Change

In the Pullman Strike of 1894, thousands of railway workers supported a strike called by the American Railway Union. The strike was forcibly and violently ended when the U.S. government brought in soldiers and the strikers rioted. It showed, however, that unions had become powerful enough to shut down an industry and have an impact on the whole nation.

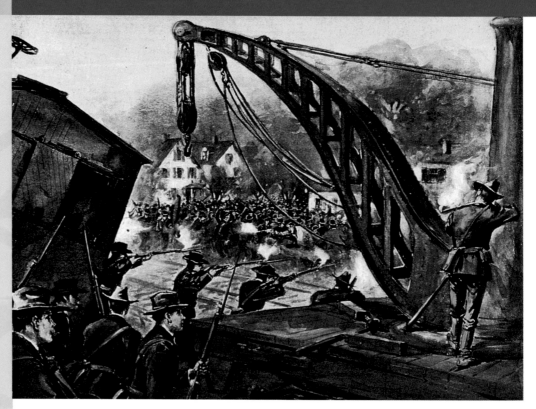

The Growth of Unions

American factory workers knew owners were making huge profits from the hard labor of their employees and that they had no intention of using those profits to improve working conditions and pay. There were those in the working class, however, who were determined not to be powerless. **Unions**—which represent working people and fight for improvements on their behalf—had existed in America as early as the 1700s, but they had mostly been small. If unions were going to make a difference, they needed many more members and had to connect working people to one another.

In the late nineteenth century, the union movement grew stronger. The establishment of the American Federation of Labor (AFL) in 1886 brought together several separate unions, and their combined strength grew to more than a million workers by the 1890s. Under the leadership of Samuel Gompers, the AFL concentrated on getting better working conditions for its members, pushing for shorter working days, higher pay, and better conditions.

Women Remain Unrepresented

The earlier unions usually excluded women workers for several reasons. They considered women to be unskilled workers, and many men did not want women involved in the workplace at all. Women were denied the chance to join the few unions that had negotiated improvements in wages and hours for their members. In 1865, women workers, with the help of reformers, formed the Working Women's Protective Union. For many years it was one of the few organizations that helped working women.

Samuel Gompers (1850—1924)

Samuel Gompers was a key figure in the labor union movement. Born in England, Gompers worked with his father as a cigarmaker from a young age. He came to the United States in 1863, when he was thirteen years old. The next year, he joined the Cigarmakers' Union, and by 1877, he was its president. In 1886, Gompers helped create a confederation of several different unions called the American Federation of Labor, an organization that fought to improve working conditions. Gompers avoided the political battles in which so many unions became involved. He concentrated on practical issues instead, such as improved pay and shorter hours. After the Triangle fire, he was chosen to be on the Factory Investigating Commission created to reform working conditions in New York factories. Except for one year, Gompers was president of the AFL until his death in 1924.

More Women in the Workforce

The end of the nineteenth century was a time of change for women. More of them had jobs than ever before, and by 1895, there were 5 million working women in the United States. More unions began to accept women, and new women's unions were forming. Many female workers joined unions in secret, so their bosses would not find out. By the early 1900s, more than half of all union members in the **garment** industry—clothes-making businesses— were women.

In 1900, several women's garment unions combined to form one organization. It was called the International Ladies' Garment Workers' Union (ILGWU), and it worked to protect the rights of female clothes makers. An all-women's labor union formed in 1903, the Women's Trade Union League (WTUL), and it was a combination of poor workers seeking better working conditions and wealthy women reformers who supported them and campaigned for women's **suffrage**. The WTUL held public meetings

A typical garment workshop around 1900. This large room full of workers at long tables is similar to the workrooms in the Triangle factory, where the fire broke out in 1911.

calling for reform, and they attempted to organize women garment workers in New York City.

Shirtwaist Workers Go on Strike

In spite of the growing union movement, working conditions did not change much, and garment workers became increasingly angry and frustrated at working in dangerous conditions for little pay. By 1909, more than thirty thousand people, most of them women, worked in New York City's five hundred shirtwaist factories.

The Triangle Waist Company was the largest shirtwaist-making company in New York and the one least willing to improve its workplace. On November 9, 1909, five hundred workers at the Triangle factory went on strike. Two weeks later, as the strike continued, shirtwaist workers held a meeting in the Cooper Union hall to determine what to do next. Many people gave speeches, and the women decided it was time to act. They voted for a general strike of shirtwaist workers. The next day, over twenty thousand garment

On the evening of November 22, 1909, women filled the Cooper Union hall in New York City. They voted for a general strike of shirtwaist makers to support the Triangle factory workers already on strike.

workers from hundreds of workshops went on strike. Known as the "Uprising of the Twenty Thousand," it was the first large-scale strike of women workers in the United States.

On the Picket Line

Shirtwaist workers **picketed** all day outside New York City's factories. They marched and carried signs demanding that owners

Rules for Pickets

"Don't walk in groups of more than two or three.

Don't stand in front of the shop; walk up and down the block.

Don't stop the person you wish to talk to; walk alongside of him.

Don't get excited and shout when you are talking.

Don't put your hand on the person you are speaking to. Don't touch his sleeve or button. This may be construed as a "technical assault."

Don't call anyone **"scab"** or use abusive language of any kind.

Plead, persuade, appeal, but do not threaten.

If a policeman arrests you and you are sure that you have committed no offence, take down his number and give it to your union officers."

From a leaflet issued by the Ladies' Shirtwaist Makers Union

Strikers outside their workplace in February 1910.

improve the factories. Not only did the women suffer from the cold, but they were attacked and beaten by men hired by the factory owners. They were also harassed and arrested by police and then fined or sent to jail.

The strikers were demanding several things. They wanted better pay and union recognition. They wanted fire escapes and shorter working days. At first, the factory owners were not willing to give in to these demands, and the strike continued into 1910. It was very hard on the families of striking workers. The WTUL helped the women by collecting money and food for them. Some wealthy members of New York society picketed with the striking women. This attracted more publicity to the cause, and the newspapers and public began supporting the workers.

The Strike Comes to an End

By February 1910, most companies had given in and agreed to a shorter workweek, higher wages, and paid holidays. The shirtwaist strike officially ended on February 15. The strike was a huge success for shirtwaist workers overall but not for the Triangle workers. The Triangle factory's owners never

Help Not Wanted
"If the strike is won, it will be on its merits, not because it was assisted by wealthy ladies. . . . They will harm the labor movement, which, to be successful, must be entirely independent."

Union activist Emma Goldman, who objected to the help of rich supporters of the striking shirtwaist workers

Passing the Building Code

Amazingly, the Triangle factory had passed the building code requirements of the time. The Asch building in which it was housed had been finished in 1901. It was 135 feet (41 meters) tall and—being under 150 feet (46 m) tall—was allowed to have trim and floors made of wood instead of more fireproof metal. The building code did require buildings of that size to have three staircases, and the Asch building only had two. The stairwells were so small that doors had to open inward to workrooms, something that was forbidden by the building code because it was dangerous in an emergency. New York City's Building and Fire Departments ignored these imperfections and approved the building anyway.

One of the two staircases that served the entire Asch building—it was the only one that some workers could reach when fire broke out because the doors to the other stairway were locked.

There was no sprinkler system to put out fires with water, and the fire escape only went down to the second floor, 20 feet (6 m) above the ground. Worst of all, the wooden doors that led to the staircases from the Triangle workrooms were locked from the outside during working hours so the employees could not steal anything and sneak off. The women had asked for this practice to be stopped, but the factory owners continued to lock them in.

gave in. The Triangle employees went back to work when the other shirtwaist workers did, but nothing had changed. They still worked fifty-nine hours a week for the same pay as before, and the factory had not been improved at all.

Inspections

One of the requests the striking Triangle workers had made was for an improvement in fire safety. There had been four fires at the Asch building in the ten years before the strike, but nothing had been done to make the factory safer.

In 1909, a fire prevention expert inspected the Triangle factory. He recommended the factory begin practicing fire drills. He also strongly suggested that the company stop locking employees in and encouraged the owners to do something about overcrowding on its three floors. The Triangle factory owners ignored these recommendations.

A fireman inspected the Asch building during a routine visit in October 1910, just a few months before the fire. He reported that the fire escape and stairways were good and that the building was fireproof. The fireman also mentioned that there was a 5,000-gallon (19,000-liter) water tank on the roof, and there were 259 pails of water scattered throughout the building. He believed these precautions would be sufficient to fight a fire in the case of an emergency.

The fire in 1911 broke out on the eighth floor of the Asch building, where the sign reading "Triangle Waist Company" hangs. The Triangle factory occupied the eighth, ninth, and tenth floors. Other companies rented space on lower floors.

21

Fire

Fire Breaks Out

The Triangle fire began between 4:30 and 4:45 P.M. on March 25, 1911. The other companies in the building had already sent their employees home for the day, but there were still close to five hundred Triangle workers in the factory. It is uncertain how the fire actually started, but it began in the cutting room on the eighth floor.

The fire spread very quickly, devouring piles of fabric, tissue paper, and cloth scraps left all over the room. The workers and supervisors attempted in vain to put out the fire by throwing several pails of water on the flames, but the fire only continued to grow. Workers found a fire hose and turned it on, but no water came out. They realized they had better stop trying to fight the fire and focus on getting out alive.

The Asch building had no fire alarms. Realizing the workers on the upper floors would have no warning of the fire, Triangle employee Dinah Lifschitz on the eighth floor tried to get through to

A typical cutting room in the early 1900s has rolls of fabrics stacked up (left) and a floor littered with fabric scraps. The rolls and scraps were piled high in the Triangle factory, helping the fire spread rapidly.

them. Before leaving her desk, she called up to the ninth and tenth floors, but only reached someone on the tenth.

On the Eighth Floor

Some workers on the eighth floor escaped down the stairs on the Greene Street side before the fire engulfed that stairwell. Several groups managed to get down in the elevators, sometimes with more than thirty workers crowded into one car.

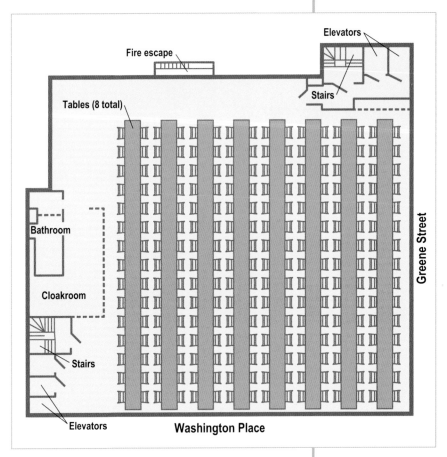

A floor plan of the ninth-floor workroom—the middle floor of the Triangle factory's three stories at the top of the Asch building—shows how 240 sewing stations were squeezed around eight long tables. Chairs and work-baskets made it impossible to get out except by climbing over the tables.

A Warning Ignored

On November 25, 1910, four months before the Triangle fire, a factory in Newark, New Jersey, caught on fire. Workers were trapped in the building, and twenty-five people died. New York City Fire Chief Edward Croker warned that the same sort of thing could happen in his city. He told local newspapers, "A fire in the daytime would be accompanied by terrible loss of life."

One person who read Croker's words was a professor at New York University, and he immediately wrote a letter to the New York City Building Department. He said he could see crowded and unsafe conditions in the Asch building across from his classroom window. The city assured him there would be an investigation into the situation, but nothing was done to prevent the impending catastrophe.

When the ninth-floor workers tried to leave after fire broke out, they found themselves locked in. This illustration published after the fire shows an artist's image of the women inside the workroom as flames engulf them.

THE LOCKED DOOR!

The fire was closing in and the eighth-floor workers panicked. Women and girls jammed up against the door on the Washington Place side of the cutting room. This made it impossible for them to open the door, which opened inward, until one worker pushed his way through and pulled the door open.

Some workers crawled out of the windows and onto the fire escape, where they slipped and fell down to the sixth floor. Someone broke a sixth-floor window and they all climbed back inside. They were trapped there by locked interior doors, but fortunately the fire had not yet spread to the sixth floor.

On the Tenth Floor

As the fire reached the tenth floor, Triangle factory supervisors took control. They quickly guided the frantic workers to the elevators and stairways and got them away from the windows. Soon, however, all paths leading down to safety were cut off by fire. Instead, people had to push their way through the smoke up to the roof. Among these were the owners of the Triangle factory, Isaac Harris and Max Blanck, along with two of Blanck's young children. They and a number of workers who made it to the roof climbed over to the adjoining buildings.

The Factory Owners

Max Blanck and Isaac Harris

Within the garment industry, Max Blanck and Isaac Harris were known as the "shirt-waist kings." They opened the Triangle factory in the Asch building in 1902, and by 1908, they had produced over one million shirtwaists.

Both Blanck and Harris were shrewd businessmen. Harris was in charge of running the factory—he would often walk up and down the aisles during business hours to check that the work was being completed to his standards. Blanck was more friendly and personable than Harris, and he was in charge of marketing and selling.

After the fire, the newspapers attacked Blanck and Harris, but the bad publicity did little to affect their profits. Their business and public life continued as if unaffected by the event. They moved the Triangle Waist Company out of the burned Asch building to other premises and continued making money from shirtwaists.

The tenth floor suffered few losses because people were warned and because they could escape onto the roof. There were close to seventy people on the tenth floor when the fire broke out, and only one died, a young woman who jumped from a window before anyone could stop her.

A newspaper montage of photographs shows the horror of the fire: the collapsed fire escape (left) that hurled people to their death; the burned wreckage (top right) of the ninth and tenth floors; and the broken elevator (bottom right) after workers fell into the deep hole of the shaft.

On the Ninth Floor

No one had managed to warn the 250 workers on the ninth floor. The workers had gathered their coats from the cloakroom when they saw flames breaking in the windows. They started screaming and running to the doors, but the managers had locked the door on the Washington Place side. The Greene Street staircase was quickly cut off by fire, and not very many workers escaped that way.

In the thick smoke and confusion, many groups of women were pushing against each other, trying to find a way out. Some gathered around the elevators, waiting for them to come back up. The elevator shaft was open, and several people in front of it were shoved into the gaping hole. They plunged to their death, and their bodies jammed the elevators.

One of the women in the workroom was able to break a window, and dozens rushed out onto the fire escape. Some ran down the escape and re-entered the building on the sixth floor. But then

Falling Bodies

"We came tearing down Washington Square East and made the turn into Washington Place. The first thing I saw was a man's body come crashing down through the sidewalk shed of the school building. We kept going. We turned into Greene Street and began to stretch in our hoses. The bodies were hitting around us."

Frank Rubino, New York City firefighter

the rickety fire escape—unable to handle the weight of so many people—collapsed, hurling workers into the street below.

Firefighters Arrive

The elevators were jammed, fire had cut off the stairways, and the fire escape had collapsed. But there was some help on the way. A policeman ran into the building and let out the women trapped behind the locked doors on the sixth floor. Firefighters arrived on the scene six minutes after the fire started and immediately stormed into the building. They battled the flames in the stairwell, trying to work their way up to the employees trapped on the upper floors.

Help from Neighbors

When the fire broke out in the Asch building, a law class was being held on the tenth floor of the New York University building opposite, on Washington Place. The students ran up to the roof, where they found some ladders left by workers. They placed ladders between the university's roof and the roof of the Asch building above

When the firefighters arrived, they found their ladders would not reach to the top of the Asch building. They aimed their hoses as high as they would go in an attempt to dampen the flames on the upper floors.

the Triangle factory. Some students led frantic people across the ladders to safety, while others pulled trapped Triangle workers up from the tenth floor on the Greene Street side.

Trapped

Many people on the ninth floor were still desperately seeking a way to escape. For them, there was only one way out. Outside, firemen held out brand new safety nets as the workers jumped from the windows, but the force of so many people hitting the nets at once broke the nets. The women

Leaping out of buildings onto safety nets was sometimes the only way to escape fires, as shown in this picture from the 1890s. The Triangle workers jumped bravely, but the nets failed to save them.

Doctors and police examine Triangle fire victims on the sidewalk after they had jumped from many stories above. They did find some survivors, but most people died from their injuries.

died falling through the nets onto the sidewalk. The firefighters then put a ladder against the building, but it only reached up to the sixth floor, many feet below where the trapped workers watched in terror.

Some of the firefighters tried to get to the workers by climbing up on the outside of the building. They could not reach them, and there was not enough time anyway. The fire closed in on the trapped workers and they couldn't bear it any longer. Dozens of girls and women and several men began jumping from the window ledges of the ninth floor. Some desperately attempted to grab at the ladder rungs, but they missed and fell past the firemen to the street below.

Plunging to Death

The workers jumped from the ninth floor knowing they would die. They tied pieces of cloth around their eyes and walked off the ledge or held hands and made the plunge together as a group. The crowds watching below wailed and sobbed as more and more workers fell to their deaths.

Seen From Below
"A young man helped a girl to the window sill. Then he held her out, deliberately away from the building and let her drop. . . . He held out a second girl the same way and let her drop. . . . Then he held out a third. . . . I saw his face before they covered it. You could see in it that he was a real man. He had done his best. We found out later that, in the room in which he stood, many girls were being burned to death by the flames."

William G. Shepherd, eyewitness and United Press reporter, March 27, 1911

Stories of Heroism

Pauline Grossman, a Triangle worker, told newspaper reporters that three of the male workers caught in the fire made a bridge with their bodies. They swung themselves across a narrow alleyway to a building on the Greene Street side. Several people escaped by climbing over the men's bodies and into the next building. Grossman told the reporter, "As the people crossing upon the human bridge crowded more and more over the men's bodies, the weight upon the body of the center man became too great and his back was broken." According to her account, the other two men then lost their grip and fell along with the people crossing at the time. It is not known if this really happened, but there is no doubt that many people acted heroically to help others that day.

Inside the building, the firemen finally reached the ninth floor and chopped down the doors. They began spraying the fire and within a half-hour had put it out. But it was far too late, and no one was found alive on the upper floors. The police found thirty-six dead workers in an elevator shaft. Nineteen charred bodies were found against the locked doors, and twenty-five dead workers were crowded together in a cloakroom. But it was the sixty-two people who

There were so many dead bodies that a temporary morgue was opened in a building on the Twenty-sixth Street pier. People filed by the coffins looking for missing relatives. After six days, seven bodies were still unclaimed.

jumped to their deaths that made the Triangle fire burn on in the minds of the public.

Identifying the Dead

The police had to push back crowds of onlookers as they began taking the dead bodies away. People in the crowd wanted to see if any of the victims were their relatives or friends. Thousands of people followed the police wagons to the **morgue**, where they walked through the rows of bodies attempting to identify friends and family. This was a horrible experience for people, some of whom lost more than one immediate family member. The police eventually identified all but seven of the 146 victims of the fire.

A Funeral March

A week after the fire, a funeral was held for the seven unnamed victims. On April 5, 1911—a cold, rainy day—over 120,000 people marched through New York City in honor of the dead. Businesses in the area closed, and the city grieved for several days.

A flower-filled carriage makes its way through a crowd of thousands on April 5, 1911. It was followed by hearses carrying the seven unidentified bodies to the cemetery. Jewish, Protestant, and Catholic funeral services were held so that all the likely faiths of the victims were acknowledged.

Chapter 4

After the Fire

Women mourn after hearing they have lost a relative in the fire. Some families, already desperately poor, would find it impossible to survive after losing daughters, sisters, or both.

Life Is Cheap

"Every week I must learn of the untimely death of one of my sister workers. Every year thousands of us are maimed. The life of men and women is so cheap and property is so sacred. . . . I know from my experience it is up to the working people to save themselves. The only way they can save themselves is by a strong working-class movement."

Rose Schneiderman, union activist, speaking at a meeting, New York City, April 2, 1911

Relief Effort

Immediately after the fire, the City of New York organized a massive relief effort for the victims' families. The citizens donated $120,000, which was a very large amount of money in 1911. The Red Cross and the ILGWU decided how to use the money most effectively. Instead of giving the same sum to each family, they tried to help some by giving them money to start a business and others by buying tickets for family members in Europe to come to the United States. Some money was used to send grieving family members back to Europe.

Who Was to Blame?

The victims' families and friends were suffering, but they were also very angry. Newspapers began criticizing the factory owners and the government for not preventing the fire at the Triangle factory. They demanded that someone be held responsible for the deaths of so many young workers. One journalist was outraged at the owners' offer to pay the families of the dead workers one week's wages, writing that it was "as though it were summer and they are giving them a vacation!"

Nobody Takes Responsibility

Even as the smoke from the fire cleared, different governmental departments began defending their innocence. The Building Department made it clear it had performed its duty by making sure the factory met standard building code. The Fire Department explained that it was not

Obeying the Law

"I have obeyed the law to the letter. There was not one detail of the construction of my building that was not submitted to the Building and Fire Departments. Every detail was approved and the Fire Marshall congratulated me."

Joseph Asch, owner of the Asch building, March 25, 1911

Angry public opinion was reflected and encouraged by equally angry words in the newspapers. Pictures, such as the two on this *New York Evening Journal* front page, told as much as any words.

responsible because it did not have any power to make owners install safety features.

The Trial of Blanck and Harris

After the fire, Triangle factory owners Blanck and Harris began a campaign to defend their public image. The public was not fooled by the owners' attempts to clear their names, however, and continued to pressure for their arrest.

On April 11, 1911, Max Blanck and Isaac Harris were charged with **manslaughter**. The trial did not begin until eight months later, and by this time, some had forgotten about the tragedy. The victims' families had not forgotten, however, and at the trial they rushed at Blanck and Harris, yelling "Murderers! Murderers!"

During the trial, the prosecutor called more than one hundred witnesses, most of whom were survivors of the fire. These workers testified repeatedly that the doors in the factory had been locked. The defense argued that so many workers died because they did not react quickly or intelligently during the fire. The **district attorney**

Jury members listen to a Triangle employee give her account of the fire. During the eighteen days of the manslaughter trial, witnesses talked about how the fire started and what happened when it did.

INSPECTOR OF BUILDINGS!

RECORD FIRE
FOR NEW YORK
145
LIVES **LOST**!!!!
BUILDING FIRE PROOF
ONLY FIRE ESCAPE
COLLAPSES.
O.K. INSPECTOR

INSPECTOR
OF
BUILDINGS

Everyone claimed they were innocent, including the New York City Building Department that had allowed the dangerous Asch building to pass inspection. The cartoonist who drew this picture at the time obviously thought otherwise.

tried to convince the **jurors** that people died because of Blanck and Harris's **negligence** and disregard for their workers' lives.

The Verdict

To find Blanck and Harris guilty, the judge said, the jury had to believe beyond doubt that the owners knew the doors were locked on the day of the fire. The jury deliberated for an hour and fifty minutes before returning a verdict of not guilty. The court had made it impossible for the jury to convict the Triangle owners

Rose Schneiderman (1882—1972)

Rose Schneiderman was born in Poland and moved at the age of six to the United States, where she was raised in orphanages. In 1903, she founded the Jewish Socialist United Cloth Hat and Cap Makers Union and went on to become vice president of the New York WTUL in 1907. During the shirtwaist strike, Schneiderman picketed with the workers and was arrested. After the Triangle fire, she made a famous speech, saying that change should come through an uprising of the working class. Schneiderman became president of the national WTUL in 1926, was appointed secretary of the New York State Department of Labor, and became an advisor on labor issues to President Franklin D. Roosevelt. Schneiderman supported the cause of working people until her death in 1972.

because there was no absolute proof that the owners knew the doors were locked.

The district attorney tried again—this time, Blanck and Harris were charged with the manslaughter of the seven victims who remained unidentified. But the case was dismissed on the instructions of the judge.

The Public Demands Change

Blanck and Harris were never convicted of any crimes connected to the Triangle fire. After the fire, they collected $65,000 from insurance companies and reopened the Triangle factory in another building. People were outraged that the court system could or would not do anything to punish those responsible, and they began to call for change. The public did not want the workers of the Triangle Factory to have died in vain. If the law could not punish

This Is One of a Hundred Murdered
Is any one to be punished for this?

Newspaper illustrations such as this one made the government realize that the issue of safety in factories was not going to go away. Public opinion demanded regulation of the workplace.

those responsible or prevent this from happening again, then the law needed to be changed.

The day after the fire, the unions created a committee to investigate problems in factories and to list possible solutions. The Committee on Safety used a questionnaire to find out what the problems were. They asked factory workers questions in private so they could not be punished for answering honestly. They asked them things like, "In your shop or factory, are the doors locked?" and "Are there fire escapes on all floors?" The committee was determined to prevent another tragedy like the Triangle fire.

Not Responsible

"The fault in New York City is that there is nobody responsible for anything. The Fire Department is not responsible; the Building Department is not responsible; the Police Department is not responsible; the Health Department is not responsible. If anything happens they are all [avoiding responsiblity]. . . . The Asch building fire started with the Fire Department. The Fire Department says, 'Our records are all right; everything we ordered was complied with.' The Building Department says, 'Our records are all right.' The Health Department says, 'Our records are all right.' The Police Department have not got through investigating yet, and I don't think they ever will and nobody is responsible. There are just as many factories in New York in the same condition as the Asch building was and probably is today."

Edward Croker, New York City Fire Chief, first public hearing of the Factory Investigating Commission, New York City, October 10, 1911

Chapter 5

Reform

The Progressive Era

At the time of the Triangle factory fire, the United States was dealing with new issues such as the growth of cities, industrialization, and immigration. The Progressive Era, as it became known, was a time of drastic change in the United States and American society. The period lasted roughly from 1890 to 1920, and it was a time when Americans were developing **legislation** and social **reform** to meet the changing times. People fought for all kinds of causes, including women's suffrage and rights for working people.

During the Progressive Era, the unions tried to use the power of striking workers to fight for better working conditions. This was a long uphill struggle,

Suffragettes were women who campaigned for the right to vote. The suffragettes shown here are marching in the Labor Day parade in 1911, the year of the Triangle factory fire.

The Right to Live

"What the woman who labors wants is the right to live, not simply exist— the right to life as the rich woman has the right to life, and the sun and music and art. You have nothing that the humblest worker has not a right to have also. The worker must have bread, but she must have roses, too. Help, you women of privilege, give her the ballot to fight with."

Rose Schneiderman, Cleveland, Ohio, 1912

but the Triangle fire had made an impact. Soon, society's attitudes began to change.

The Government Responds

The public outcry after the fire had an effect. Within a few months of the fire, New York City passed the Sullivan-Hooey Law in October 1911, creating the Bureau of Fire Prevention. The fire commissioner was given new powers, and the Fire Department hired several hundred inspectors who could demand immediate improvements.

Even before the Sullivan-Hooey Law, the Committee on Safety asked the New York state **legislature** to create a government commission to investigate factory conditions as a whole. On June 30, 1911, the legislature passed a law creating the Factory Investigating Commission to inspect factories in the state of New York. The group was charged with investigating fire prevention, unsanitary conditions, workers' hours, ventilation, and health problems caused by the workplace.

The goal of the Commission—whose nine members included AFL president Samuel Gompers and WTUL leader Mary Dreier—

After the Triangle fire, the WTUL, shown here, was active in investigating safety in the workplace and campaigning for improvements. The New York legislature appointed Mary Dreier, president of the New York chapter of the WTUL, to the Factory Investigating Commission.

In this New York factory, men are operating lathes with no safety devices. The Factory Investigating Commission visited hundreds of factories such as this one with the aim of improving the dangerous conditions it found.

was to prevent another Triangle fire and to improve the everyday life of workers. This was an important step forward for the state's poor working people.

The Commission Gets to Work

The Commission plunged itself into discovering the truth about New York's working conditions. Rose Schneiderman and many other investigators inspected factories throughout the state. Several factory owners voluntarily made changes to their premises after being made aware of the problems. Many of them had never actually walked through their own factories.

The Commission required people to testify at its hearings. Hundreds of factory workers did so, with unbelievable accounts of terrible conditions within the workplace. Fire prevention experts and government fire officers also testified before the Commission. They said that more than half of the fires within factories could be prevented with a stricter fire code.

Results

Between 1911 and 1914, the New York state legislature passed thirty-six new laws at the suggestion of the

Factory Investigating Commission, changing almost every aspect of factory life. Companies now had to become licensed with the government, reporting what kind of business they operated and how many people they employed. New laws limited how long women and children could work and prohibited them from working at night. The Commission suggested several reform measures concerning the fire code. It said smoking in factories should be banned, sprinkler systems should be installed in buildings with more than seven floors, and fire drills should be practiced in all factories.

These reforms were only the beginning. The creation of the Factory Investigating Commission in New York State provoked many other states to form commissions. The entire nation went on to pass many labor laws and continues to do so today.

Labor Day

The first Labor Day, created to honor working people, was celebrated on September 5, 1882, in New York City. The Central Labor Union planned the event, including a parade and festival to entertain working people and their families. In 1884, the holiday moved to the first

The first Labor Day parade passes through Union Square in New York City in September 1882.

Monday in September. With the growth of labor organizations, the holiday was soon observed in several industrial cities. On June 28, 1894, Congress passed an act making Labor Day an official holiday that is still celebrated every year in the United States.

Conclusion

The Brown building as it appeared in 2003. Once a place of tragedy, it is today part of a university campus and subject to many safety regulations.

A Monument to the Dead

"The greatest monument we can raise to the memory of our 146 dead is a system of legislation which will make such deaths hereafter impossible."

Morris Hillquit,
former sweatshop worker

The Building

The building that held the Triangle factory is still standing in New York City. It is now called the Brown building and has been designated as a national historic landmark. The building is used by New York University for classrooms and offices. If it were to catch fire today, those inside would be able to escape. They would have the help of fire escapes, sprinklers, and fire drills, thanks to the reforms that took place after the Triangle fire.

Labor Today

Because of the pioneering work of the Factory Investigating Commission, the government still regulates working conditions in factories. The long struggle between labor and business continues, however. Business owners continue to operate **sweatshops** that the government does not know about, often staffed by illegal immigrants unaware of their rights. These shops have horrible working conditions similar to those during the Industrial Revolution. Workers in some businesses, including the garment industry, continue to be paid far less than is needed for a minimum standard of living, even though they work long hours at exhausting jobs.

The power of unions to demand change has declined since their peak in the first half of the twentieth century. This is partly because the nature of work has changed—as machines take over many manufacturing jobs, the workforce has moved from factories into service industries, where unions have less influence. As a result, today it is the workers in low-paid service jobs—such as those in hotels, restaurants, and large retail stores—who often find themselves in the poorest working conditions.

An ILGWU plaque commemorates the site of the Triangle fire. In this picture, a garment worker stands in front of the plaque with a wreath placed there by UNITE (the Union of Needletrades, Industrial, and Textile Employees), which replaced the ILGWU in 1995.

The Legacy of the Triangle Shirtwaist Factory Fire

The long-term effects of the Triangle fire are still felt today. Before the Triangle fire, workers in city factories lived in a virtual state of slavery, unable to demand change. Unchecked, owners would sacrifice the health and safety of their workers in their pursuit of money. The unions were trying to improve the situation, but they could not fight big business on their own.

The Triangle fire had a huge impact on the public because they witnessed the horrible deaths of young, innocent women. As a result, the government was pulled into the battle between organized labor and big business. Factories became regulated and workers gained many rights. The Triangle factory workers unknowingly gave their lives so that workers in the future might gain the right to demand safety in the workplace.

Time Line

1793	Cotton gin, invented by Eli Whitney, begins to be used.
1800	Eli Whitney makes first interchangeable parts.
1865	Civil War ends.
	Working Women's Protective Union is founded in New York City.
1882	September 5: First Labor Day parade.
1886	American Federation of Labor (AFL) is founded.
1894	Congress declares Labor Day an official holiday.
1900	Several garment trades combine to create the International Ladies' Garment Workers' Union (ILGWU).
1901	January 15: Construction of Asch building is completed.
1902	Triangle Shirtwaist Company opens factory at the top of Asch building.
1903	The Women's Trade Union League (WTUL) is formed.
1909	Fire prevention expert recommends improvements in fire safety at Triangle factory, none of which is implemented.
	November: Shirtwaist workers in New York City go on strike.
1910	February 15: Shirtwaist strike ends.
	October 15: Asch building passes routine fire inspection.
	November 25: Fire kills twenty-five workers at a factory in Newark, New Jersey.
1911	March 25: Fire kills 146 people at the Triangle factory.
	April 5: Thousands of people attend funeral march for unnamed fire victims in New York City.
	April 11: Isaac Harris and Max Blanck are charged with manslaughter.
	June 30: New York State Factory Investigating Commission is created.
	October: Sullivan-Hooey Law creates Bureau of Fire Prevention in New York City.
	December 5: Harris and Blanck trial begins.
	December 27: Harris and Blanck are found not guilty of manslaughter.

Glossary

district attorney: legal representative of a district in a city or county.

garment: piece of clothing.

immigrant: person who comes to a new country to make his or her home.

industrialization: change from an agricultural way of life to one based on manufacturing and other large industries.

juror: person who sits on a jury in a court of law.

legislation: deciding and enacting of laws.

legislature: group of officials that makes laws.

malnourished: suffering from not getting enough nutritious food.

manslaughter: crime of unintentionally causing the death of another person, less serious than murder.

morgue: place where dead bodies are taken for examination or if they are unclaimed.

negligence: carelessness or lack of attention to duties.

picket: make a protest outside a place, such as when workers protest outside their place of employment.

reform: make changes designed to improve conditions.

reformer: person who campaigns for or introduces reforms.

regulate: control employment or other practices with regulations or laws.

scab: term used by strikers for a person who is hired in place of a striking worker; or who goes to work at his or her workplace in spite of a strike; or who crosses a picket line to do business when a strike is in progress.

strike: work stoppage in protest at working conditions or employers' actions.

suffrage: right to vote.

sweatshop: crowded factory with bad working conditions.

tenement: apartment house usually in a poor part of a city.

textile: fabric that has been woven or knitted.

union: organization that campaigns and negotiates for better working conditions for its members, who are usually workers from a particular trade or area of business.

unsanitary: so dirty as to be unhealthy.

urban: having to do with a city.

ventilation: access to fresh air.

workhouse: place where people were sent for punishment, like prison but for less serious crimes.

Further Information

Books

Freedman, Russell. *Kids at Work: Lewis Hine and the Crusade Against Child Labor*. Clarion, 1998.

Goldin, Barbara Diamond. *Fire! The Beginnings of the Labor Movement* (Once Upon America). Puffin, 1997.

Gourley, Catherine. *Good Girl Work: Factories, Sweatshops, and How Women Changed Their Role in the American Workforce*. Millbrook, 1999.

McCormick, Anita Louise. *The Industrial Revolution* (In American History). Enslow, 1998.

Stanley, Jerry. *Big Annie of Calumet: A True Story of the Industrial Revolution*. Crown, 1996.

Stein, Conrad R. *The Pullman Strike and the Labor Movement* (In American History). Enslow, 2001.

Streissguth, Thomas. *Legendary Labor Leaders* (Profiles). Oliver Press, 1998.

Web Sites

www.ilr.cornell.edu/trianglefire/ The School of Industrial and Labor Relations at Cornell University has an excellent online exhibition about the Triangle fire.

www.uniteunion.org Information for students about the campaign against sweatshops provided by UNITE, the present-day garment workers' union that replaced the ILGWU. Also has a kids' page where the topic of child labor is explored.

www.uniteunion.org/research/history/historyinaction.html Information about and pictures of women who led the reform movement in the garment industry.

Useful Addresses

American Labor Museum
Botto House National Landmark
83 Norwood Street
Haledon, NJ 07508
Telephone: (973) 595-7953

Index

Page numbers in *italics* indicate maps and diagrams. Page numbers in **bold** indicate other illustrations.